The Conspiracy Against the Dollar

By the same author

THE
CONSPIRACY
AGAINST
THE DOLLAR

The Spirit
of the New Imperialism

PETER BETER

George Braziller　　　*New York*

Standard Book Number: 0–8076–0709–6, cloth
0–8076–0710–X, paper
Library of Congress Catalog Card Number: 73–79850
First Printing
Printed in the United States of America
DESIGNED BY VINCENT TORRE

TO

my wife *Lilly*

and our children

Alexander Mathias and *Josée-Marie Elizabeth*

CONTENTS

FOREWORD

9

1

GEOSTRATEGY

21

2

ECONOSTRATEGY

39

3

ECONOPOLITICS

65

4

STAGFLATION

79

EPILOGUE

99

INDEX

105

FOREWORD

T HREE generations of the Rockefeller dynasty have given over one billion dollars to philanthropy. This amount, however, is only a very small portion of the immense Rockefeller holdings.

For the most part, the third generation (and now also the fourth) have forgotten the tough, sharp, predatory business practices of the first. They have lost the taste of battle for glory—with one notable exception, the present leader of the dynasty.

The elder John D. Rockefeller created the largest scale of dynastic power in the modern world. More than any of his contemporaries he succeeded in carving out of the wilderness of America an empire so vast, so wealthy, so solidly entrenched that none dared to resist it. He became, in truth, a ruler of "royal" authority, the founder of a dynasty.

That dynasty and that empire are today in the hands of the leader of the third generation. He is the youngest, the most scholarly, the one who preeminently has retained the qualities of the elder Rockefeller, and who understands ancestral prestige.

It is true that other members of the third generation

(and also one of the fourth) have become well known in America. They, however, have only been princes of provinces (governors of states), or dilettantes. They do not share in the leadership of the family because there can be only one leader, who represents the group feelings of the dynasty. It is he who is host to heads of state and it is he who in turn visits them. And just as the founder of the dynasty was imbued with the spirit of imperialism, he too, as trustee of the dynasty, is motivated by the same spirit.

However, it is not America he is trying to carve out as an empire—this had already been done by the elder Rockefeller. It is much more.

If the leader is to do "much more," he will need the support of client followers. A dynasty depends on the quantitative and qualitative strength of such supporters. And their group-feeling strength.

This group feeling means willingness to work with and fight for each other since they have the same aims, the same opinions, the same goals.

In the eyes of the law in America, corporations are "persons." These corporate persons are client followers of the "royal" family. They form the corporate aristocracy, the supporters of the dynasty. Examples of the corporate aristocracy are GM, IBM, Ford, Unilever, Royal Dutch/Shell, ITT, to name a few.

There are other client followers, and they are to be found at home in the executive machinery of the American government, and abroad as affiliates of the U.S.-based corporate aristocracy. These are the client followers of the corporate aristocracy, and only secondarily of the dynasty.

Even the corporate aristocracy cannot enter the inner sanctum; this is reserved for the members of the "royal" family. It can, however, occupy a position in the shadow of power, close to the center. After all, the dynasty in its third generation needs the support of the corporate aristocracy. Members of this aristocracy lend money to the coffers of the dynasty which, in turn, relends it to other members, and so on. They also protect one another from attacks from outsiders now that the dynasty is spreading out from the shores of America to Europe and beyond.

Many scheme to be a part of this corporate aristocracy but only a few are admitted. If they are from families in banking, finance, or control large—though not major —corporations, they have a chance to be a part of this group.

They would have a better chance, however, if they first served in the executive machinery of the American government. Such persons look to the corporate aristocracy for leadership and when they have served it well, they may be rewarded with a position within the aristocracy. This is how it maintains its hold over the executive machinery of the government.

The corporate aristocracy needs the help of these smaller client followers, who, in turn, are only too willing to help. Examples of such client followers are the Connallys, the Dillons, the Volckers, the Haldemans, the Shultzes, the Zieglers, and varied "professors," among others. Some, like the Nixons and the Kissingers, are client followers of both the dynasty and the corporate aristocracy.

The client followers, big and small, parody the ways of the "royal" family and energetically support the dynasty, acquiring in the process the air of nobility with all of its attendant power and authority.

Like the third generation of the family, they are far removed from the time when the dynasty was first established, and unfamiliar with the difficulties that had to be overcome by the founder. They only know that it is rich and powerful, and they bow down before its monumental buildings constructed in the name of the dynasty.

Now the dynasty and its client followers are engaged in a crusade under the banner: "Spirit of the New Imperialism." Planting their banner on the shores of Europe and beyond, they aim to control the destiny of the new world of trade, using the American dollar as a tactical weapon. If the dollar becomes a casualty then capitalism itself will have been destroyed, and Lenin proved right when he wrote that "the final stage of capitalism is imperialism."

It is said that "capitalism," to quote David Rockefeller, "is a highly evolutionary and flexible concept. That the true nature of capitalism lacks ideological purity and that that is a positive opportunity rather than a negative problem. Indeed, the greatest strength of capitalism is probably its adaptability. Having the virtue of relative freedom, it is able to respond to changing circumstances more readily than tightly controlled systems. The capacity of this flexible system to deal relatively quickly with new problems is of particular importance when we look to the future. Keeping capitalism up to date will amply challenge this innate flexibility in the years ahead."

David Rockefeller is the youngest grandson of the elder John D. Rockefeller, and board chairman of Chase Manhattan Bank, N.A. It is upon him that the "royal" mantle has fallen. He is today the leader of the Rockefeller dynasty.

If the elder Rockefeller were to read his grandson's statement, would he agree that capitalism is an "evolutionary and flexible concept"? Would he ask: Is this the Spirit of the New Imperialism speaking?

Also: Into what is capitalism evolving? And in the process of evolving, will it destroy private property? The gold cover for the dollar? The dollar itself? The profit motive which has been the prime generating force behind economic growth since the Industrial Revolution?

And further, he might ask: Are you not over-extending yourself in time, space, and holdings? Have you forgotten that a dynasty is stronger at its center than at its outer limits? You must surely know, for you were well taught by my son, that when a dynasty has reached its farthest expansion, it begins to weaken.

David Rockefeller graduated from Harvard with a B.S. degree in 1936, studied a year at the Rockefeller-supported London School of Economics, and earned his Ph.D. in economics at the Rockefeller-founded University of Chicago. Before he became president of Chase in

1961, he was the least conspicuous of the Rockefeller brothers, grandsons of the world's richest man. Of the five, however, only he, the youngest, followed his grandfather into the business world.

His father, John Davidson Rockefeller, Jr., was a stern man who endeavored to instill in his sons the responsibility of being a Rockefeller: that they were very, very rich put a heavy burden on their shoulders, and many would want to be friends with them. To educate them to the real world of business and government, he would boast: "I cheat my boys every chance I get; I want them sharp. I trade with the boys and skin them and just beat them every time I can. I want to make them sharp."

As president of Chase, David Rockefeller concentrated on international matters, and as chairman and chief executive since 1969 he has continued his interest in this field. In addition to being on the boards of many family-owned or controlled corporations, he is a trustee and vice president of the Council on Foreign Relations, "a nonprofit institution devoted to the study of political, economic, and strategic problems as related to American foreign policy." The Council is also a resting place between jobs for the client followers of the corporate aristocracy. Many members have served in the executive machinery of the federal government.

Financial liaison, links, or interlocking relationships usually mean personal links, too. Bankers are found on boards of industry and even on foreign bank boards. Industry, in turn, is represented on boards of banks and even on boards of foreign industry.

There exists among them all a certain group feeling,

perhaps a superior group feeling. They are the "go-betweens" of the corporate aristocracy.

There are also "go-betweens" linking the corporate aristocracy and members of the executive machinery of the federal government; these are the client followers of the corporate aristocracy, as previously mentioned.

An example of the first group of "go-betweens" is Sir John Hugo J. Loudon of London. He is chairman of the international advisory committee of Chase Manhattan Bank, N.A., and a board member of the Chase Manhattan Corporation (which controls Chase Manhattan Bank, N.A.). At the same time he is chairman, Royal Dutch Petroleum Company and Shell Petroleum N.V. (The Hague), as well as director, Shell Petroleum Co., Ltd., and trustee, Ford Foundation. Royal Dutch/Shell is ranked number one among the 500 corporations of Europe.

Another example of the first group is Willard C. Butcher. He is a director of Chase Manhattan Corporation, president and director of Chase Manhattan Overseas Banking Corporation, a director of Nederlandsche Crediet Bank N.V., Amsterdam, and treasurer of the Museum of Modern Art of New York, of which David Rockefeller is a trustee and chairman of the board.

Other examples of the same group: Herbert P. Patterson, president, chief administrative officer, and board member of Chase Manhattan Bank, a director of the executive committee of American Machine and Foundry Co., and a trustee, Brookings Institution;

William R. Hewlett, a board member of Chase Manhattan Bank, and president and board member of Hewlett-Packard Co., Palo Alto, California, director of Kern County Land Co., FMC Corp., Chrysler Corp., and trustee RAND Corp.;

Ralph Lazarus, board member of Chase Manhattan Bank; chairman, Federated Department Stores; director, Scott Paper Company, General Electric Co., trustee, Committee for Economic Development, member of National Committee on US-China Relations, Inc.

The remaining directors of Chase forge links leading out into insurance, oil, foreign relations, engineering, telecommunications, chemicals, and so forth. It is interlocking in depth. Whether any laws have been violated is not the subject of this book.

Members of the second group of "go-betweens" usually come from the stables of such Rockefeller-controlled or founded institutions as the Rockefeller Foundations, Council on Foreign Relations, and the University of Chicago, among others.

Some examples of this group are: C. Douglas Dillon, former Secretary of the Treasury of the United States, a trustee and chairman of the Rockefeller Foundation and a former director of Chase Manhattan Bank. He is now chairman, U.S. and Foreign Securities Corp., and chairman of the executive committee, Dillon, Read & Co.;

Peter M. Flanigan, President Nixon's executive director of the White House council on international economic policy and assistant to the president. He was vice-president of Dillon, Read & Co. for many years;

Steven Lazarus, director of the Commerce Department's East-West trade bureau. He is, among other things, a "good friend" of Ralph Lazarus;

18

Paul A. Volcker, undersecretary of the Treasury for monetary affairs. He came from Chase Manhattan Bank.

Secretary of the Treasury George P. Schultz was professor of industrial relations at the Rockefeller-founded University of Chicago, where David Rockefeller received his Ph.D. in economics. He is also a "close friend" of George Meany, one of the elder labor leaders in America.

Dr. Henry Kissinger came from the Rockefeller Foundation, and was foreign policy adviser to Governor Nelson Rockefeller. Foreign policy, of course, rightfully belongs to the federal government and not to princes of provinces.

Dr. Frank Stanton, former vice-chairman of Columbia Broadcasting System and an expert in electronic journalism. A trustee of the Rockefeller Foundation, he contributes to the "good image" of the dynasty.

The most imposing example of this second group of "go-betweens" is President Nixon himself. He moved from his home state of California where he could not win an election for the governorship, to New York City. There he moved into the apartment building where Governor Rockefeller lived. They became close friends but it was not until later, after his election in 1968, that his "talents" were fully and forcefully utilized.

1

GEOSTRATEGY

In the winter of 1972–3 the news was dominated by the "dollar crisis." Finance ministers of the major trading nations including Japan met in Europe to discuss ways of supporting the American dollar.

But why had the Americans refused to help the Europeans to support the U.S. dollar in this monetary upheaval? If the finance ministers were puzzled, so too were the American people. Had they not been told by their president that the dollar was a good bet? Yet, it bought less and less. Surely something was ravaging the dollar. What had happened?

The dollar had been at peace with the world for over a quarter of a century. Its health had been sound. It had been tied to gold by a solemn international agreement, had been the linchpin of the currencies of the Western world. It had been considered a "hard" currency, accepted everywhere. As long as people knew there was gold, or at least some gold, behind their dollar, they had confidence in it. In short, it was as good as gold.

America had held most of the world's gold stock after the end of World War II. The war-ravaged countries had neither gold nor dollars. The United States had come to their assistance, furnishing gifts, loans, credits, and Marshall Plan Aid. It encouraged the export of private and public capital, and it lowered its own tariff barriers.

America had become the ideal creditor. Even the gold which had been sent to the U.S. for safekeeping during the war had been returned to Europe.

In the ensuing twenty years Europe was occupied with the restoration and development of its economy, as was Japan. Assisting Europe in this restoration was the multinational corporation. It brought capital, new management techniques, and modern technology.

A multinational corporation usually denotes an American corporation with direct investments abroad. These investments as a rule take the form of a foreign affiliate incorporated abroad. There may be many foreign affiliates of a U.S.-based corporation such as IBM, GM, Ford, and ITT. These affiliates sell in more than one country and also obtain their raw materials and capital, and produce their goods in several countries. About 200 giant U.S.-based corporations are regarded as being multinational in scope. Their affiliates are client followers of their U.S.-based corporate aristocracies.

The development of the multinationals began in the late nineteen-forties. The movement was led by American corporations which saw rich new markets, especially in a Europe busy rebuilding its war-torn economy.

It also was an opportunity for the American corporations to produce cheaply abroad for sale in America. After a product has been manufactured in America and is found to be a success, the company thinks in terms of costs. If it finds that the product would cost less to produce abroad, it proceeds accordingly, even though the American worker will be out of a job. In the long-term time frame, this is what is happening all over America. The jobs, in effect, have been exported and, with them, the technical know-how.

Labor unions have been helpless to prevent or even guide this new development. They could join with multinational unions abroad only to be thwarted again, however, when the multinationals move their European or other plants to Africa and Latin America where there is a waiting labor market.

The multinational corporations with direct investments abroad increased to more than $8 billion in 1950 to more than $20 billion in 1960, and to more than $60 billion in 1971 in Europe alone. Most of this investment in Europe was centered in such fast-growing, non-extractive industries as computers, branches of electronic components, the automobile industry, chemicals, canning, pharmaceuticals, and telecommunications.

By 1972, the U.S.-based corporate aristocracy controlled 80 percent of Europe's electronic data-processing, one-third of its refining capacity, and 50 percent of its industrial semiconductors market. It accounted for some 90 percent of all outside investment.

Its client followers, the multinational affiliates, were beginning to cause grave concern in Europe. Europeans saw how these affiliates acquired or eliminated many medium and small companies, becoming larger and larger as they progressed. Their concentration in certain industrial sectors could lead to an oligopolistic market domination with resulting inefficiencies. Europe, therefore, began to warn the multinationals that they would have to curb their investments and their appetite for acquisitions in certain sectors of industry.

Meanwhile the forces of the New Imperialism were working under a five-year plan. One aspect of the plan was to demonetize gold—to sever the dollar from gold. Another was to dominate the industrial base of Europe and thus control its destiny. Still another was to use a dominated Europe for future East-West trade. And finally to do away with the international monetary agreement forged at Bretton Woods in 1944.

To demonetize gold meant to sever it as backing for the American dollar, the reserve currency for all the currencies of the Western world. Once this was done then the dollar would be a "soft" dollar, and gold would become a commodity.

The opening of the first five-year plan began during the 1967/1968 period. In late 1967 the corporate aristocracy caused their affiliates to dump billions of dollars and other currencies on the London gold market. The price of gold began to rise. Worried finance ministers of Europe, through their central banks, began to support the official price of gold by selling off a part of their own gold reserves. They lost billions of dollars worth of gold this way. However, by March 1968, they could no longer support the official price of gold on a cooperative basis. The forces against them were too great.

The United States government refused to cooperate with the Europeans to stop this run on gold. As a result, the price of gold had broken away from the fixed price of $35 an ounce. There was now a genuine "free" market price for gold. The official stocks of gold held by the central banks had become, in effect, frozen, and gold was now on its way to becoming demonetized according to plan.

The finance ministers met in Washington and agreed to confirm that there now existed a two-tier gold market system. This agreement was dated March 17, 1968, and five years later, March 16, 1973, to the year, the dollar would be severed from gold! The end of one aspect of the first five-year plan.

In theory, official gold could be used in official transactions; however, who would want to dissipate gold when a free market price was going up and up, and Europe had been told by the United States government not to turn in its excess dollars for gold?

Any central banker of Europe who sold off any part of the official gold stock of his country, or who did not add to his supply of official gold after this 1967/1968 affair would have been figuratively hanged. The people of his country looked to him to protect the value of their money.

Since Europe could not turn in its excess dollars to the United States for gold, then American dollars in Europe had become, in effect, frozen. So that by 1968 both dollars and gold had, in effect, become frozen!

Few in Europe suspected that the forces of the New Imperialism were not interested in supporting the official price of gold in 1967/1968, or that it wanted the dollar to be devalued into a "soft" currency, or that it wanted gold to be demonetized.

Europe remembered that President Kennedy had said

the "United States official price of gold can and will be maintained at $35 an ounce." But the forces controlling his administration were already at work to sever the dollar from gold. A former British Ambassador to the United States (1948–1952) stated that: "The United States should set free for 'effective use' the gold now locked up as backing for Federal Reserve notes and deposits." As if this were not sufficient advice, he remarked that the British had taken such a step twenty years ago and it had not contributed to inflation.

Immediately after he made these statements in 1960 he was appointed a trustee of the Rockefeller Foundation. He served as such until 1970. When he made the above statements, however, he was chairman of the Lloyds Bank Ltd., London. It would be to him that the representatives of the New Imperialism would look for strategy in the implementation of the five-year master plan. His name: Sir (now Baron) Oliver Franks.

Shortly after President Kennedy took office in 1961, legislation was introduced in the United States Congress (H.R. 6900) to abolish the 25 percent gold backing for Federal Reserve notes and deposits of member banks of the Federal Reserve System.

This legislation was introduced at the request and support of the then Secretary of the Treasury, C. Douglas Dillon. He was the real power in the Kennedy Administration; no important appointment was made during the Kennedy years without his consent. He planned pressure by the mass media, both printed and electronic, to be put on Kennedy when he could not or would not make up his mind, or when he did not want to cooperate.

In the end, Dillon usually got his way. But, he himself, like Sir Oliver, was only a client follower of the dynasty and the corporate aristocracy.

Opposition to the legislation to abolish the gold cover for the dollar was mounting. Led by the American Gold Association and the Western mining interests, among others, Secretary Dillon retreated and no hearings were held, though scheduled.

Dillon, with his own client supporters, had not, however, abandoned hope. They would attack at a later time. Their next opportunity would come ten years later, and then the approach would be subtle and ingenious.

In the Old World system of monetary theories, the economist would expound at great length on international financial and economic matters in terms of vague technical data, often incorrect, which the press would dutifully print. Some economists would even receive Nobel Prizes for their "equations," although there was hardly a rational individual who could understand what they were expounding, and the world economic situation continued to grow worse. They had forgotten that what man could create, he could also destroy.

In the past, international monetary affairs appeared always to be conducted in an atmosphere of cooperation, assurance, and confidence. The finance ministers and their central bankers always exuded confidence and their people felt reassured.

If things sometimes went out of balance, the finance ministers could still be confident that the economic system would balance itself out. They would accomplish this either by digging into their cash or gold reserves or adopting some monetary method, such as raising or lowering interest rates, supply of money, and so forth. Thus the economy could keep running until its trade balances would be in line again.

But this Old World system had become obsolete. It had been replaced by a new system which the economists seemed to have overlooked. They kept reiterating the same equations and figures over and over. If the United States government made a pronouncement, it must be true: The balance of payments and trade . . . They were in deficit . . . The United States is buying more from abroad than it is selling abroad. . . . It is paying out more than it is taking in from abroad. . . . Until this condition is corrected there can be no convertibility of the dollar. . . . And so forth.

The Old World system had become obsolete because of the new era of the multinational corporations and banks. They had drastically changed the nature of world trade. They had caused gross misinterpretations in the international trade picture, had taken advantage of the obsolete theory of the balance of trade and payments for their own purposes.

The affiliates of the U.S.-based multinational corporations are incorporated abroad, in Europe for the most part. As a result of long experience with American and European law they have learned to manipulate figures on exports, imports, prices, and dividends within the internal corporate shuttle. Ultimately, what was reported to the United States government as imports and exports was, to an ever-increasing extent, the result of intracorporate shuttle operations for the private advantage of the corporate aristocracy.

Here is how this shuttle operates within the framework of two U.S.-based corporations and their affiliates abroad.

Chrysler-U.S. produces and ships a front fender to its affiliate Chrysler-France. There the fender is welded onto the Chrysler 180 automobile. Because of intense competition in France it cannot be profitably sold and it is shipped to another affiliate, Chrysler-South Africa. There it cannot be sold either and is abandoned in the rains to deteriorate.

Ford-U.S. makes a front fender and ships it to its affiliate Ford-France. There the fender is welded onto a chassis which, in turn, is shipped to another affiliate Ford-Zaire for assembly into a Ford Granada, which, in turn, is shipped to another affiliate, Ford-South Africa, for eventual sale.

The transactions in these shuttle operations generally would be reported in the different country accounts as sales and purchases. They would be considered part of the trade in the world markets. There are, however, no real sales until the final one to a consumer, not to an affiliate. The transactions become part of the multinational corporations' very complicated internal accounting strategy.

These multinational shuttle operations are the devices by which U.S.-based corporations export and import capital, taking their profits and avoiding taxes. They have accumulated billions of dollars and assets and other currencies abroad in such a manner. They have been able to make huge and increasing investments in Europe. They can defer American taxes on foreign income until they are ultimately brought back to America. They receive full credit for taxes paid abroad. Past experience has shown that only as much as is required by law to pay dividends to American stockholders is ever brought back to the United States.

The sales of the affiliates of the U.S.-based corporations have been more than twice the volume of exports from America. Some of these sales have been to America as well as foreign markets. In both instances they have displaced American production and employment.

Substantially more than half of all American foreign trade is conducted between U.S.-based corporations and their affiliates abroad. And such trade is increasing significantly with each passing year. Should it continue at such a rate, America would become a service-oriented economy.

If the multinationals have learned to manipulate facts and figures, they have also learned to massage the money markets of Europe. By their sheer weight, they can unbalance market forces—as they did in the gold crisis in 1967/1968—by moving only small portions of their liquidity into and out of gold at huge profits to themselves. They had tested the waters from time to time and found they could cause waves of speculative fever.

Then: Campaign May.

It happened on signal. It was May 1971. The affiliates of the multinationals, armed with dollars, opened their Spring offensive. They dropped bombs of dollars on Europe. The Europeans, as they had attempted in 1967/

1968, tried again to rescue the American dollar. The multinationals sent waves and waves of dollars against the central bankers until these bankers were compelled to stop supporting the dollar by giving out high fixed-price currencies. The time had come to think of their own currencies and what they were doing to their own economies.

The dollar began to "float." It had become free from a fixed-rate in relation to other European currencies. It had, in effect, become devalued, "softer."

The client followers, the affiliates of the U.S.-based corporate aristocracy, withdrew to their respective treasurer offices for the reckoning.

The United States government under control of the forces of the New Imperialism, as in the gold crisis of 1967/1968, did nothing to support its own dollar. No one suspected that the government wanted the U.S. dollar to be devalued, to be turned into "soft" currency.

The dollar had become an expendable casualty of the New Imperialism.

Before this monetary crisis was over, huge volumes of newly-printed European currencies found their way into their local economies. The central banks had to have greater quantities printed to buy up the inflated dollars and, in so doing, the new local money fed the engine of inflation and social unrest in Europe. "Campaign May" would eventually cause the American people to suffer the effects of these inflationary waves.

After "Campaign May" the pace of takeovers by the multinationals of major European companies quickened. There was not much consideration given to the "mix" of the mergers or the acquisitions. Some of the attempted takeovers failed, however. One was H. J. Heinz's attempt to take over Grey-Poup-on-Maille; another, Westinghouse Electric's bid for Jeumont-Schneider; another, ITT's design for Guinard.

England had warned the Americans that she would not tolerate any majority interest acquisitions in the motor industry, computers, aircraft, and agricultural machinery sectors. Holland, however, took a liberal position, undoubtedly influenced by its two largest multinationals, Royal Dutch/Shell and Unilever. Holland participates in these two multinationals with Britain. They, in turn, are client followers of the Rockefeller-owned Chase Manhattan Corporation and its International Advisory Committee.

Two weeks prior to Campaign May, a well-guarded three-day secret meeting was held at the Rockefeller-owned Woodstock Inn in Vermont. Security was tight and the meeting had to be held outside Europe. Present with David Rockefeller and Henry Kissinger among others was Prince Bernhard of The Netherlands. Prince Bernhard is very influential in Royal Dutch/Shell, Unilever, and Societé Génerale de Belgique.

Karl Schiller, former finance minister of West Germany, identified Royal Dutch/Shell, Unilever, GM, Ford, and IBM as front line culprits in the monetary crisis.

On reflection and study, Campaign May had showed Europe that the forces of the New Imperialism were now openly bent on dominating its key economic sectors (over which elected authorities have only minimal control). The message was coming through loud and clear: The Europeans would be enslaved and the U.S.-based corporate aristocracy would hold the whip.

The Europeans would attempt to retaliate by using their antitrust laws, but the corporate aristocracy in America would cause the executive machinery of the United States government to proclaim: Discrimination against American companies! Discrimination! This alone would suffice and the Europeans would retreat.

To continue the offensive of acquiring more European companies, the multinationals needed more "soft" dollars. "Buy cheap—sell high" is the usual rule, but in this case it was "never sell—hang on." In any event, the dollar had to be deflated further if the affiliates in Europe were to do the job for the corporate aristocracy back home in Amerca.

These major multinationals had learned earlier how to massage the money markets. They were not at all speculators. They held all the cards. They knew they could win and therefore took no risk. They had more resources than all of Europe together. Nothing, it seemed, could stop them; they had the support of the most powerful forces in Amerca.

The new European money system was uncontrolled and its existence was generally unnoticed. Hence, the affiliates in Europe could dominate this new money system for the corporate aristocracy. Generally, they used American-controlled-or-influenced banks in London and elsewhere to place buy-and-sell orders with European foreign-exchange dealers. The latter do not—as a rule—state publicly on whose behalf the orders come, but they do "arrange" for the finance ministers to know.

When the multinationals are sometimes queried as to what they are up to, they invariably respond with the usual line that they do not "speculate" in currencies "at all" and that they do need foreign currencies from time to time to pay or prepay debts due in foreign currencies. Of course they do not speculate.

An American president of a major multinational in Brussels states: "Since the Europeans are making us pay dearly for their national defense, they may as well turn it [Europe] over to us. It will eventually be dominated by us so we can play trade with the Russians. If we pull our forces out of here, they will be left to the missiles of the Russians. So they [Europeans] had better grow up."

"Yes, we are grateful to America for helping us to regain our territory during the war and for America's assistance after the war," countered a former European finance minister, "but: the war is over! What do you want from us now?"

Said an American banker in London: "We have already made the world believe that the visible U.S. export trade has been going down in relation to the export trade of other countries. This could be used as an excuse to push exports, but better still, it could be used to devalue the dollar. Thus we could export more products."

Another in London added: "The only way, and I mean the only real way, you are going to devalue the dollar is to sever it from gold. Once this is done, you are free and clear. There is no sense in asking these European countries to upvalue their currencies to help our exports. They have their farmers to think about and they can be very difficult, especially in election years. Anyhow, the multis have already taken over the export trade in America. What you want is an 'absolute divorce' of the dollar from gold. *That way there is no limit to the amount of cheap, soft dollars we could turn in for their good money. This way too we could use more of their own money in profits to take over their own key industries."* (Emphasis supplied.)

Of course if the dollar were severed from gold, even indirectly, the forces of the New Imperialism could also "finance" any project of any size during East-West trade relations in an uncontrolled soft currency, the American dollar.

". . . and if you look beyond these horizons [Europe], our own country [America], for the first time in our adult lifetime is finally strengthening its relationship with the Soviet Union and with the People's Republic of China," said United States Ambassador to France, Arthur K. Watson of the IBM corporate aristocracy.

Another aspect of the master plan, the first five-year plan, was on track: Use Europe as a springboard to go East to try to dominate East-West trade, and perhaps beyond.

The client followers of the corporate aristocracy would be supplied with more weapons for the immediate goal ahead: to increase the pace of takeovers of the industrial base of Europe, and hence Europe itself.

Thus, while the military establishment of the United

States was engaged in a "thirty-years' war" in Indochina for the purpose of using Indochina as a vast testing ground for its new military hardware, the New Imperialism had begun a war of its own in Europe for the control of Europe itself. Europe had become a geostrategic necessity to insure passage of exports to the East.

The larger questions were beginning to loom on the European horizon: Would the forces of the New Imperialism succeed in conquering the industrial base of the new Europe? Or would they be repulsed by the growing army of Europe's young industrialists?

Would Europe unite in time to save herself from the external threat?

Onto the stage stepped President Nixon.

2

ECONOSTRATEGY

O<small>N</small> August 15, 1971, President Nixon announced a sweeping "New Economic Program," calling for a ninety-day wage, price, and rent freeze to be effective immediately. He imposed a 10 percent surcharge on imports, ordered a 5 percent federal job cut, and postponed federal raises. He also asked Congress to repeal a 7 percent tax on automobiles, a 10 percent tax credit on new investments, and a rescheduling of an income tax cut planned for 1973 to January 1, 1972.

Sandwiched in between all this window dressing and confusion of words was the most important news: *The declaration of war against the dollar!* By executive order he officially severed the dollar from gold.

In formal language the President declared to the Western world that the United States would suspend settlement of international transactions in gold, thereby violating the 1944 international monetary agreement of Bretton Woods. *This action also had the effect of abolishing the 25 percent gold cover of the dollar.* Thus the legislation to abolish gold backing for the dollar in 1961 was approved by executive order of Nixon in 1971.

The procedure had been well contrived. The inflationary situation originally brought about earlier in Europe by the forces of the New Imperialism had begun to cause some economic dislocation in America. This comparatively insignificant state of affairs, blown out of all proportion with the help of the client-follower mass media, was used as an excuse to sever the dollar from gold. It was a part of the plan of *econostrategy*.

Econostrategy: The employment of the executive machinery of government, and all client followers, to use all available economic forces as tactical weapons for stated goals. In this instance it was the use of the executive machinery of the United States government and all client followers of the dynasty and/or the corporate aristocracy to cause massive inflows of dollars into Europe, in addition to their own, to assist their forces in the goal of the economic domination of Europe.

Just as there were inflows of billions of dollars into Europe in Campaign May in 1971, there would be substantially more dollar inflows into Europe before and after President Nixon's August 15th announcement, and increasingly more so in succeeding offensives.

This strategy was recommended to President Nixon by the then Secretary of the Treasury, John B. Connally, Jr. He, however, was only a transmission belt. He was not the architect of the plan. He had strong support from his undersecretary of the Treasury for monetary affairs, Paul A. Volcker. Mr. Volcker had fulfilled his assignment well. Prior to appointment, he was with the Rockefeller-owned Chase Manhattan Bank as a vice-president.

For his continued underlying support and loyalty, former Secretary of Treasury C. Douglas Dillon was rewarded with an appointment to the renowned Rockefeller-owned Chase Manhattan's International Advisory Committee. He was already chairman of the Rockefeller Foundation. The Rockefeller-controlled International Advisory Committee, however, has a much more powerful liaison with corporate aristocracies—worldwide.

President Nixon had said his economic freeze would be temporary. (As it turned out, it was; it proved once again that it would pay to keep an eye on the ball.) There was actually no need for an economic freeze at that time; Nixon used the occasion to sever the dollar from gold— the real objective.

The other facets of his "New Economic Program" would all disappear in a short time, for nothing really would be accomplished by them. It was distraction at its best. Later, when the forces of stagflation (high inflation combined with stagnation in the economy) would truly be rampant in the American economy he would refuse to take really effective steps to correct the situation. In any event, he had accomplished what he had been told to do and to say by his masters.

Secretary Connally was of immense help in the execution of the plan. He could bluster and attract television coverage and the press. Moreover, he had a strong and confident personality. The president had selected him to be his Secretary of the Treasury in December 1970 and it was Nixon himself who swore Connally into office February 1971.

Connally had had a very close relationship with former President Johnson. He had been his administrative assistant at one time when Johnson was a senator, and he managed Johnson's political campaign for the presidency in 1960. Connally was the only "outside" person who could fault Johnson and get away with it—as long as it was considered constructive criticism. At times the arguments between them would become heated and explosive, but in the end Johnson would relent and take Connally's forceful and useful advice.

Secretary Connally held the attention of the financial and economic groups in Europe. They had their eyes for the most part on the 10 percent surcharge because it could hinder trade relations between America and Europe. Although an element of confrontation for them, it was primarily a sop to American labor unions. Until 1965 labor in America was for the concept of free trade but when they awoke they discovered that the corporate aristocracy had moved away taking jobs and know-how with them. Only the labor leaders in the American shoe unions knew what was taking place but the other labor leaders did not listen.

In any case, soon after Nixon's declaration of war against the dollar was announced the currencies of the Western world went adrift in a sea of confusion. Dollars flowed into the central banks of Europe. It was like Campaign May again. The bankers closed their doors. The dollar was afloat.

Nixon's action of severing the dollar from gold had set in motion an inflationary force greater than America had ever experienced in the twentieth century. The momentum of this action would carry from one monetary crisis to another.

Meetings of finance ministers and their central bankers were held all over Europe. With unflinching demeanor they would issue such statements as "useful exchanges" and "constructive ideas." Connally would counter through a spokesman: "Many countries want to get back to fixed exchange rates with as little change as possible as soon as possible. This isn't satisfactory to the United States."

Client-follower Nixon wanted other countries to increase the value of their currencies, thus effecting a substantial devaluation of the American dollar, a down value in relation to other currencies, but not a devaluation tied to gold. He did not want a devaluation for the sake of trade (this was only a cover) but to assist the New Imperialism to take over Europe economically with cheap dollars.

If the European countries (and Japan) would not upvalue their currencies then Nixon wanted a completely free market where market forces would determine the value of the dollar. Should dollars pour into a country, however, the dollar would fall against the home country currency to such a low point that there would be no longer a demand for it. And should dollars pour out, the opposite effect would take place. Europe was not willing to permit that kind of float to occur. No central bank or any government, for that matter, would surrender its sovereignty to allow the free market to determine that country's monetary destiny. The finance ministers would intervene in the money markets by way of interest rate charges, fiscal measures and other controls before sur-rendering their sovereignty to the forces of the New Imperialism.

In any event, there had been little recent experience with floating currencies. It took time to arrive at any conclusions. The practical problems of a floating system are more complex than the theories of economists, but the United States government was not in a mood to budge from its position of a free float. Said Secretary Connally: "The United States hasn't any intention of changing its attitude by one iota."

This was blunt language, but was it an empty threat? The Europeans continued to intervene in the free market and prevented the United States from obtaining the an-ticipated benefits from the severance of the dollar from gold.

Meanwhile, the confusion surrounding Nixon's eco-nomic package continued in America. Economists argued about the merits and demerits of the freeze on rents and wages. Everyone became mired in minute details.

The Europeans and Japanese thought the confronta-tion had narrowed down to the 10 percent surcharge on their exported products. And in Paris, IBM's corporate-aristocracy spokesman Watson said: "Whatever you may think of the tactical approach used in August, 1971 —when an import tax was created to stimulate revalua-tions in other countries—I think you would agree that something had to be done."

But the Europeans did not agree that "something had to be done." They had done everything they could to help the United States when it cried over and over again:

"The balance of payments deficit, the balance of trade deficit of the United States . . ." This cry of wolf had fooled the Europeans into thinking the United States had such deficits; they did not yet realize that the corporate aristocracy in America and its affiliates abroad had changed the Old World economic order.

The Europeans became confused; they believed the United States had no real battle plan for meeting the situation. The monetary crisis continued until December, 1971, while the United States continued to insist that it did not want an increase in the price of gold by even a moderate amount as a concession. In other words, the United States wanted Europe to agree to upvalue their currencies in relations to the dollar so that the dollar could be devalued with no practical significance in the official relationship of the dollar to gold. The United States would not agree to a technical increase in the price of gold because it planned to completely demonetize gold.

Then, in early December, 1971, the finance ministers of the leading industrial nations met in Rome. Secretary Connally, acting as chairman of this important group, had his assistant, Paul Volcker, sit on his right. He had press handouts ready for distribution. The meetings went into "executive session," whimsically borrowed from United States Senate procedure, and as such they would be restricted solely to the finance ministers and central bank governors, causing the deputies and officials who normally are present to contemplate the cold corridors of the Palazzo Corsini.

Volcker presented the meeting with "his" plan. It would reveal that the United States had relented a little from its initial hard-line attitude on currency upvaluation. It would ask Europe and Japan to average an 11 percent upvaluation against the dollar compared with an earlier 15 percent upon which the corporate aristocracy had seemed determined.

Connally managed to sidestep a direct answer to the question of whether the United States was or was not prepared to raise the price of gold.

Dr. Karl Schiller, then the German economic minister, was the one person in all of Europe who was knowledgeable about the real situation concerning the corporate aristocracy in the United States and its affiliates and client followers in Europe. Dr. Schiller remarked: "The country on which we had all centered our hopes put forward a hypothetical offer which was much bigger than most countries expected." This was a polite way of saying what Connally had said in poker-game language: "Let's look in theory at what would happen if we devalued the dollar by, say, ten percent!"

The countries of Europe and Japan were not in a position to respond to this "generous" offer of the United States. They would need time to consult their respective governments. Connally made it obvious that he had full powers to act for President Nixon and showed his impatience. . . . "If I reflected impatience," he said, "it was the expression of an irresistible urge to speed the process of altering a monetary system that has crumbled and a trading system that is essentially inequitable." He did not go deeper to ask who was responsible for the monetary system to become "crumbled." It appeared to be shallow thinking, and to compensate for his lack of insight he was sometimes accused of chauvinism and of being too tough in negotiations.

At the close of the Rome meeting Connally invited the assembled group to meet again in two weeks in Washington for further talks. Perhaps by that time Nixon's forces would offer a carrot in the form of a new offer to placate the interested parties. Perhaps they would welcome a carrot but they were still in no mood to allow the United States to reshape the international monetary system to its own design.

Immediately following the Rome meeting, the value of the dollar in relation to other currencies dropped to record lows on foreign markets. It was a reaction to Conally's "hypothetical" question.

The group of finance ministers reassembled in the Smithsonian Institution in Washington in mid-December, 1971. Connally had gone to great lengths to find a suitable place to hold this "historic" meeting.

He was in a much better frame of mind at this meeting and so too were the assembled participants. He had an experienced hand to assist him in the negotiations: David Rockefeller, the leader of the dynasty. Mr. Rockefeller was present and active to make sure nothing went wrong this time.

As a result, the ten richest industrial powers outside the Communist world agreed to an 8.57 percent devaluation of the dollar, and it would be accomplished by a $3 increase in the price of gold from the old price of $35 an ounce. The United States had backed down on its position of devaluing the dollar without any reference to gold. But this position was not to last very long.

Nixon hailed the agreement, which provided for the first devaluation, as "the most significant monetary agreement in the history of the world." Whether this was for domestic or world consumption would not matter for both had become accustomed to such hyperbole from him or his followers. After all, had not most of the president's assistants in the White House come from the advertising world?

The devaluation was designed to make U.S. goods more competitive in the world market, according to Connally. Statements such as this would be made after each subsequent devaluation.

As part of the devaluation agreement, the United States suspended the ten percent import surcharge that the president had imposed with much vehemence on "foreign" products imported into the United States.

The parties had compromised. The dollar still remained a reserve currency because it was defined in terms of gold, though both were "frozen." The dollar was in the twilight zone. Hardly anyone now knew what constituted the dollar. Yet, because it was still a reserve currency, it helped the multinational affiliates in their offensive to take over the industrial base of Europe.

The takeover pace was stepped up, but the going was beginning to become difficult. Warnings of one kind or another were given to the multinational affiliates by all the European countries. They would be restricted to certain sectors of the economy, they would have to submit to searching accounting procedures, they would be watched to see if they "unbalanced" the national economies. Most important of all, if the multinational affiliates wanted their stock to be listed on the European stock exchanges, they would have to submit more documents, usually in the national language, full information about current business, and future intentions. Europe was now in no mood to be trifled with. Its nervousness had already been increased dramatically following numerous politically distasteful acquisitons, so-called "stealing" of national resources by the multinational affiliates. So Europe was now aware. Measures had to be taken.

In order to placate certain sectors of the European economy and at the same time to prepare the ground for further offensives, the leader of the dynasty and his client followers, the corporate aristocracy, arranged to meet at a place and setting befitting their "royal" station in life. The conference would be held at the Palace of Versailles, in Paris, March 1972.

The Palace of Versailles is the usual location for meetings of heads of state or diplomats. This time the guests would be the leader of the dynasty, the corporate aristocracy, and their client followers. They represented assets well over $300 billion, more than the combined assets of the countries of Western Europe! The forces of the New Imperialism had, in effect, reached the level of a private centralized state, but without an army.

The meetings had the aura of an important diplomatic Congress. Some of the members of the corporate aristocracy present were General Motors, General Electric, Exxon, Atlantic Richfield, Royal Dutch/Shell, Indiana Standard, IBM, Caterpillar Tractor, H. J. Heinz, Xerox, ITT, du Pont, Kodak, Goodyear, Merck, Pfizer, Westinghouse. David Rockefeller and his controlled-or-influenced banks were present as well as client followers of these banks.

The meetings were not open to the public; econostrategy, East-West trade, and Europe were discussed.

Chase Manhattan Bank informed the participants about progress concerning its opening of a branch office in Moscow and its hope to open a "liaison office" in the People's Republic of China sometime in 1973. Chase would be the first U.S. bank to supply credits on its own, and also through the U.S. government-owned Export-Import Bank for this East-West trade. Only those companies cooperating with the Spirit of the New Imperialism would get financing.

Chase's Paris office had been in the forefront in financing grains and other commodities with the Eastern bloc countries during the sixties, mostly through the assistance of the Export-Import Bank of the United States. Now Chase was pushing natural gas and other energy projects in the Soviet Union and the Eastern bloc countries. It would need the cooperation of all the client followers present. Declared an intrigued observer: "The fascinating aspect of this growth of East-West trade is that it will occur to a significant degree through the good offices of and with money drawn on a Rockefeller bank."

The largest multinational bank, Orion Bank, Ltd., was founded in 1970 by Chase Manhattan, Royal Bank of Canada, Britain's National Westminster Bank, Westdeutsche Landesbank Girozentrale, Credito Italiano, and Mitsubishi Bank. Orion is represented in more than 100 countries, with headquarters in London. It is a Rockefeller bank. Any request for an international loan originating in Europe—for example, in Dusseldorf's West-deutsche Landesbank Girozentrale—is first telexed to the National Westminster Bank and then on to Chase Manhattan in New York for "instructions"—or interest. Orion Bank was well represented at the meeting held at the Palace of Versailles.

Two months after the Versailles meeting, Connally resigned as secretary of the Treasury. About two weeks prior to his resignation, on Sunday, April 30, 1972, he feted President Nixon at a lavish barbecue at his ranch at Floresville, Texas. Three times governor of Texas and the only Democrat in the Nixon administration, Connally praised the Republican chief executive in words usually reserved for campaign rallies: "I respect this particular president of the United States for the manner in which he conducts himself." Nixon responded: "John Connally . . . is, in my view, a man who has demonstrated he is capable of holding any job in the United States that he would like to pursue. I am just glad he is not seeking the Democratic nomination."

At the barbecue were over 200 members of the U.S. corporate aristocracy. Most all had come in their corporate jets. The skies trembled as the planes roared to a landing in the ranch's newly reconstructed 4,100 foot strip. Each arriving guest was personally introduced to President Nixon by Connally in a formal reception in the ranch's high-ceilinged livng room. Later, guests rose to drink a toast with French champagne to "the courage of the president." Connally was described by Nixon as the "dynamic and skilled architect" of his "new economic policy," when in truth, he was not; he merely played a key role in selling this one facet of econostrategy to the public at large. It had come to the point that no one knew who was using whom!

Connally had always dreamed of big money connections. While former President Johnson concentrated on gaining political power, his protégé, Connally, would concentrate on gaining economic power. And economic power was present at his ranch that day. In fact, a great part of the economic power of the corporate aristocracy is today centered in Texas and in oil. Among those present at this gathering of the clan of the U.S.-based corporate aristocracy were construction magnate George Brown of Brown & Root, Fort Worth oilman W. A. Moncrief, Dallas billionaire H. Ross Perot, N. Bunker Hunt of the Hunt Oil empire, as well as John Murchison of industrial and banking fame, Ima Hogg (Houston millionairess), Fort Worth Perry Bass, a co-executor with Connally of the famous Sid Richardson Estate (where Connally first made his big money contacts).

Four months after the Versailles meeting, Connally became head of "Democrats for Nixon." (He became a Republican officially on May 2, 1973.)

One member of this political group was Thomas J. Watson, Jr., chairman of the executive committee of the IBM corporate aristocracy, a trustee of the Rockefeller Foundation and a member of the Council on Foreign Relations. Another was John T. Connor, chairman of the board of Allied Chemical Corporation, a director of Chase Manhattan Bank and also member of the Council on Foreign Relations.

It was election year in the United States. The forces

of the New Imperialism would have to turn their time and energies to help their client follower be reelected. Europe would get a respite until after the election.

Several weeks before the November 1972 elections, however, 124 finance ministers leisurely assembled in Washington to discuss monetary matters. The atmosphere had become festive and many felt they were on holiday. Had not the Smithsonian Agreement brought relative monetary peace? Were not the trading nations getting back to work?

To this happily-assembled group, Nixon declared: "We need to develop procedures for prompt and orderly adjustment of exchange rates and to create a responsive monetary system, responsive to the need for stability and openness." This was music to their ears. Here was the president speaking about "orderly adjustment of exchange rates" which for them meant there was hope that the existing machinery under the Bretton Woods agreement as to flexible exchange rates would be retained.

As if to add to this state of euphoria Secretary Schultz spoke softly, saying the United States wanted to strike a new balance in international economic affairs and that he intended to work closely and intensively with the other countries in recognition of their legitimate requirements. Further, he said, the United States had given up its policy of waiting upon events and had decided to cooperate with other powers in search of a solution to the muddle which had been created. "The United States," he said finally, "will take part in the negotiations in *a spirit of cooperation, not imperialism.*" (Emphasis added.)

David Rockefeller, who was present and who had a

hand in the negotiations of the Smithsonian Agreement, said he was pleased by President Nixon's speech to the assembled group. He felt it was more internationalist in tone—"a friendly expression." He said further that "the dollar is in a much stronger position now than it has been in a number of months." He also felt that the "positive suggestions" by Secretary Schultz had brought "a sense of purposefulness and forward movement in international monetary affairs. And I think this, too," he said, "has contributed to the strength of the dollar."

And to make sure the soothing words of Messrs. Nixon, Schultz, and Rockefeller, had made their point, the White House issued a statement quoting the president as saying further that the United States "will be prepared to take bold action with our European partners for a more equitable and open world economic order. We look to them for continued help in fostering a climate of mutual cooperation and confidence."

Nixon was sworn into office for his second term on January 20, 1973. David Rockefeller made a "goose trip" through Eastern Europe ostensibly on trade matters and hurried on to London, arriving there February 1st, where he conferred with some of his client followers. They informed him all was going well. They had resumed their offensive on the dollar. IBM and GM were supporting the forces of Ford and Unilever. Royal Dutch/Shell was busy regrouping banks and supporting their efforts.

A new monetary crisis was beginning to gain momentum. With an estimated $190 billion at their disposal, including a $2.5 billion inflow from banks in the United States to their affiliates in London and elsewhere in Europe, the major multinational affiliates, now joined by minor multinational affiliates who were playing follow the leader, hurled more than $8 billion at the doors of the European central banks. Within the week ending February 11, 1973, the central banks had had enough. They bolted their battered doors. The dollar was floating again!

The major multinational affiliates of the corporate aristocracy, who controlled twice as much money as the international reserves of all the world's industrial countries, made windfall profits estimated at $750 million. They could easily attack with less than 3 or 4 percent of available funds to set off a monetary crisis which would, in turn, lead to a devaluation of the dollar! The $2.5 billion inflow from banks in the United States would be kept in Europe for psychological reasons and would never return to the United States.

It should be observed that the client followers of the dynasty and the corporate aristocracy earned far more money on the foreign-money exchanges than by producing goods over a comparable period of time! They would use the money thus "earned" to continue their offensive in the service of the Spirit of the New Imperialism.

There was only a remnant left of the Smithsonian Agreement of December 1971. And there was not much unity left in Europe. It had received a body blow of tremendous impact.

There were hurried meetings in Europe and Japan with Paul A. Volcker. One of the president's jet planes was placed at his disposal. The client followers could not wait to devalue the dollar again.

Then, February 1, 1973, the United States announced that the dollar would be devalued. Secretary Schultz said this second devaluation of ten percent had "no practical significance" in the official relationship of the dollar to gold! He added: "We remain strongly of the opinion that orderly arrangements must be negotiated to facilitate the continuing reduction of the role of gold in international monetary affairs."

It would take one more "crisis" to demonetize gold.

As if on cue, Schultz echoed the words of former Secretary Connally after the first devaluation: "There can be no doubt we have achieved a major improvement in the competitive position of American business."

Schultz, as noted above, was careful to point out that there was no relationship of the dollar to gold. Gold, in his eyes, had been reduced to a mere commodity, like the metals in the United States national stockpile: tin, copper, lead, and zinc, among others, to be sold off in the course of time.

If such commodities were sold off, the commodity market prices in the short term would suffer but in the long-run the outlook would be very bullish. In a demonetized gold system, whoever bought gold would hold on to it and then sell a few ounces whenever the price soared again. The more the American dollar cheapened, the more the price of gold would increase in value. As for the other commodities, there would perhaps be a financial gain of some proportions to the United States but the econopolitics effect would be felt for a very long time around the world. Those producing countries in Latin America and East Asia which operate their extractive industries as state enterprises would suffer the most; those industries owned by the U.S.-based multinational corporations would suffer the least, if at all.

By waiting until Nixon had been reelected, the forces of the New Imperialism had regained the ground they had given up in the first devaluation. The dollar previously had a relationship to gold; now, in this second devaluation, the dollar had a vague relationship to gold —to something called "paper gold." "Paper gold" is only paper, and there is no confidence in paper. The dollar was now in a halfway house.

Before the U.S. Congress could officially confirm this second devaluation, on February 22, 1973 another offensive against the dollar was made by the client followers of the corporate aristocracy. They were not going to give Europe a breathing spell this time! Another crisis!

The client followers zeroed in on the German D-mark. They bought up enormous quantities of D-marks with full knowledge it would be revalued upward, meaning they would later be able to sell the D-marks they bought for more than they paid for them. This is how they would make their profit.

Another front was opened. This time the client followers bought gold with their available resources. Its price on the free London bullion market soared to $90 an ounce! The dollar's value on Europe's foreign exchange markets weakened considerably.

As if Europe needed one more body blow to knock it to the floor, on March 1, there came another offensive by the client followers. Europe was awash in a sea of dollars. The central banks again were forced to bolt their much-battered doors. The dollar weakened further, yet the next day, President Nixon would say that he regarded the dollar as "a good bet in the world markets today." Asked if he would bring the "speculators under control," he replied that he "could not." This was a true answer. He was not a free agent. He had allowed himself to be owned by the forces of the New Imperialism.

Meetings were called by the finance ministers of Europe. There was no panic. They appeared stunned! The United States government watched from afar. It was not in a hurry to rush to Europe this time. "Let them stew in their own juice for a while," said a Treasury official. "When will they ever get the message: we hold the whip, they are the slaves!"

During their deliberations in Brussels or Paris or elsewhere, the finance ministers were kept busy reading the reports of their technical committees as to what to do to protect their respective monetary sovereignties. They were not in a position to counterattack and they were not in the position of holding good cards for the moment. They kept hearings voices which said "float, float." If they were going to float their currencies they had better do it together. They were playing for time but the doors of their central banks could not be kept closed indefinitely.

They had all recalled the international monetary agreement of Bretton Woods in 1944. It had provided for fixed parities or values between currencies. This system —a fixed parity system—they had remembered was to correct the monetary anarchy and the nationalism of the

1930s which prevailed at that time caused by floating rates of exchange. Bretton Woods had been brought into existence to correct such a system. Now they were being pushed back into the 1930s by the United States.

Finally on March 16, 1973, in Paris, the United States and the other major industrial countries agreed on a plan to end the third major dollar crisis since the time President Nixon had officially declared war against the dollar (August 15, 1971).

The text of the communiqué issued after their meeting indicated the major trading European currencies would remain in fixed relationship with each other, but change their value, that is, float against the dollar as one group. The United States agreed to intervene to support the dollar on the foreign money markets when it felt it was necessary. There appeared to be no fixed level agreed upon. The dollar would float against their currencies, which meant it could continue to bob up and down, up-value and devalue.

The effect of the Paris agreement was to change the monetary system which had been in force since World War II. Gold had become completely demonetized. Another aspect of the five-year plan had been completed on schedule. Now the international monetary system was afloat in dangerous waters.

Nationalism was very much alive. Even though there was a collective float, the countries of Europe were still sovereign states with separate budgets, separate central banks, separate issuing authorities, separate economies, separate political systems, separate agricultural programs, separate rates of inflation, beset by several groups of weak and strong currencies. Where was the group feeling to be found? And when?

The offensives of the New Imperialism had caused the dollar to become the first casualty. Gold had become demonetized. European unity and cooperation had taken a severe beating from these same forces. Would they be the next casualty?

Secretary Schultz had told the European bankers he would try to have interest rates raised in America in an attempt to have the excess liquidity of some $80 billion floating around Europe return to America. Some American banks actually took him at his word! Hardly had he returned to America when they raised their prime lending rates by at least half a point. The White House protested, and after five days of discussions they all bowed to its pressure and suspended their increases. Whereupon, for the sake of appearances, Chase Manhattan increased its own prime rate, but climbed down in one day, using alleged White House "pressure" as an excuse. Interest rates would later be "allowed" to rise, but would eventually be forced downward again.

Such was the situation by the end of March 1973. The goal of the New Imperialism to dominate the European economic community was continuing on track. The front-line troops had done their job well. But the job was not yet completed.

Europe had been cowed but she had not yet been dominated. The forces of the New Imperialism would turn loose their client followers, Nixon and Kissinger, into the European arena. Through their voices, Europe would hear the call to resurrect the Atlantic alliance and the old partnerships following World War II. She would also hear her defense needs linked to trade and monetary issues, with an implied threat that if she would not negotiate on these issues, America would reduce her armed forces in Europe.

Immediately after World War II, Europe had been poor, battered, and fearful of Russia. Now everything had changed. Shock tactics would no longer avail. By the end of April, 1973, Europe was grossly suspicious of America's intentions, and President Nixon's use of "defense" as blackmail to force Europe to make trade concessions would fail.

The Europeans, themselves, would regain the initiative after much soul-searching, regrouping, and reuniting. In the end, the external threat would cause them to stand firm. Meanwhile, they would continue their efforts to establish a central bank for themselves, and to erect complex trade barriers which would harass products and components of products of the corporate aristocracy manufactured either in America or Europe.

3

ECONOPOLITICS

THE New Imperialism has twin major objectives. One is to dominate Europe in every sense of the word; the other, to dominate East-West trade. Both involve the jungle of commercial competition. The first objective involves the use of multinational affiliates, dollars, and the executive machinery of the United States government as tactical economic weapons. This is econostrategy, as we have indicated.

The other is big power politicking involving the use of multinational affiliates and the executive machinery of the United States government as economic-diplomatic tactical weapons. This is *econopolitics.*

As was seen in econostrategy, the dollar was not only used directly as a tactical weapon but also indirectly. And as such, it was itself warred against, becoming the first casualty. It was severed from gold. It became an international IOU. A paper "currency."

For the "enlightened leadership" of the New Imperialism, such "currency" had become an instrument to be used in an expanding American and world economy. To Robert V. Roosa, former undersecretary of Treasury for monetary affairs (1961–64) and now trustee, and member, respectively, of the Rockefeller Foundation and Council on Foreign Relations, the main question remaining to be resolved is: What should the world use for primary reserve assets? As a client follower of the corporate aristocracy he believes it is not gold, for that would not insure "constructive flexibility" of an international monetary system. His theory is that the total value of the productive capacity of the corporate aristocracy would be sufficient to give the dollar value and confidence in the coming new world of monetary relationships.

In econopolitics, the dollar would be used indirectly as an inflated medium of exchange. This was its new role in the world of "constructive flexibility." It would not, however, be used to play its proper role as a measuring stick to measure East-West trade. Thus, the true value of East-West trade would never be correctly analyzed and so would never be known. The inflation-ridden dollar at the beginning of the fiscal year would be worth twice what its value would be at the end of such year. The result would be fictitious balance sheets with fictitious taxable profits.

On August 15, 1971 President Nixon had commenced battle against the dollar and opened the offensive in Europe. A month earlier he had made public the offensive for East-West trade. He divulged he would visit Peking in a "journey for peace."

It would be a "major development in our efforts to build a lasting peace in the world," he said. He was going "to seek the normalization of relations between the two countries and to exchange views on questions of concern to the two sides. . . . As I have pointed out on a number of occasions over the past three years, there can be no stable peace and enduring peace without the participation of the People's Republic of China and its 750 million people. That is why I have undertaken initiatives in several areas to open the door for more normal relations between the two countries."

By opening "the door" he meant the "planning," back in April 1971, of table-tennis diplomacy, easing of the twenty-year United States embargo on trade with Red China, partial restoration of telephone contact with that country, and a Nixon study group, headed by former United Nations Ambassador Henry Cabot Lodge, urging Red China be admitted to the United Nations.

Later in 1971, Mr. Nixon made it known that he would also meet with Soviet leaders in Moscow after his trip to Red China for a "working visit" with a minimum of ceremony aimed at "enhancing the prospects of world peace."

Before he was feted in China, that country had taken the place of the Nationalist Chinese in the United Nations. It should be noted here that it was the combined vote of the countries of the Third World which supported mainland China's admission into the United Nations. They were not alert to the fact that she would be taking away from them most of the benefits which were accruing to them from the specialized agencies of the United Nations, such as the Industrial Development Organization, World Health Organization, World Bank, and other UN organizations having to do with atomic energy, labor, food, education and science, economic development, children's aid, aviation, postal services, telecommunications, meteorological work, and maritime shipping. Red China was large enough to take most of them, leaving some crumbs to the others who had voted for her admission to the United Nations.

By the same token, the same thing would happen to the people of America. The United States government would earmark billions for East-West trade and deny its own citizens funds for social development projects on the ground that such projects would be "inflationary"!

In February 1972 President Nixon visited China for one week. Both parties agreed that they would try to avert the danger of international war, that neither "should seek hegemony in the Asia-Pacific region and *each is opposed to the efforts by any other country or group of countries to establish such hegemony.*" (Emphasis added.) Further, neither was "prepared to negotiate on behalf of any third party," nor would they assist each other in any operation against "other states." The clause "each is opposed to the efforts by any . . . group of countries to establish such hegemony" would be circumvented because the parties had made it applicable only to the "Asia-Pacific region."

Upon his return to America, Nixon said "there were no secret deals of any kind." This was half true. What had been agreed upon was the basis of a structure for trade.

This structure would include the establishment in the future, and under the auspices of the executive machinery of the American government, a council for trade between the two countries, dominated by the dynasty and the corporate aristocracy. Was it not for this purpose, among others, that they had been waging an economic war in

Europe? Were they then not entitled to the spoils, all the spoils: Europe and East-West trade? The council would fail because of the delays in opening direct trade talks, the failure to find experienced and willing personnel to follow through, and most important of all, because of Japanese trade missions with their super-charged economic base. Even in mundane matters they (the Japanese) would have "reserved" almost all hotel accommodations in South Korea and Hong Kong so as to prevent others from going into China. The council would only be a dream, but at least soybeans and other agricultural commodities would be "sold" along with other products, the bulk of which would be made in Europe.

In May 1972 Nixon visited the Soviet Union for a week. There was talk of pacts about missiles, health and environmental problems, joint space efforts, scientific and technical cooperation, the nuclear arms race, land-based ICBMs and submarine-launched missiles, and the freezing of offensive missile arsenals. It all sounded so complex and technical. The most important announcement, however, was their joint intent to negotiate an overall trade agreement.

This trade agreement would provide for a Soviet-American joint commercial commission and would be dominated by a client follower of the corporate aristocracy, as was the case in the proposed China-America trade council. The first urgent "sale" to be negotiated would cover enormous amounts of American wheat and other agricultural commodities totaling billions of dollars, the bulk of which Russia would store, with some going to her own

71

client followers in other countries. Russia would also request the tools to manufacture consumer products herself, and United States funds to help develop some of her oil and gas resources, the latter to be used also for bargaining purposes against the Japanese in the near future.

The Nixon visits to China and Russia were prepared by Dr. Henry Kissinger, Nixon's assistant for national security affairs. He had come into the executive machinery of the federal government from the stables of the Rockefeller-controlled Council on Foreign Relations, the Rockefeller Foundation, and as foreign policy adviser to Governor Nelson Rockefeller of New York. Therefore, he came saddled with power and could never err in the eyes of his co-client follower Nixon.

Both Nixon and Kissinger were used as "go-betweens," as traveling salesmen for the "royal" dynasty and the corporate aristocracy.

The announcement that President Nixon would visit China came as a "shock" to Japan's Prime Minister Eisaku Sato. Sato was considered to be a close friend of the president and Nixon had not taken him into his confidence long before making the announcement.

In any event, because of pressure from the "angered" Japanese public and to "save political face," Sato, whose term would have ended in October 1972, declared he would quit June 17. The minister of international trade and industry, Kakuei Tanaka, took Sato's place as Prime Minister.

Unnoticed by the world press was a previous secret invitation by China for opening diplomatic relations with Japan. Her idea was to use Japan to block Russia's efforts to extend its influence in East Asia. After Nixon's announcement of his visit to China, and using this announcement as a public excuse, Tanaka lost no time in accepting China's invitation.

He expressed regret and repentance to Premier Chou En-lai for his country's past aggression. In September 1972, both countries signed an accord to end the technical state of war which had existed between them since 1937. As a result, ambassadors would be exchanged within six months' time; there would be the opening of embassy offices in both capitals (and to oblige the Red Chinese, the Japanese would turn over the Nationalist Chinese embassy buildings in Tokyo), the exchange of goodwill and commercial missions, negotiations for an air transport agreement, a fishing pact, a commercial agreement, and a peace treaty ending World War II. China was making things very easy for Japan because she wanted Japanese industrial know-how from automobile manufacture to atomic power, among other things.

Premier Tanaka accepted China's position that the government of Taiwan is an "inalienable part of the People's Republic of China" but did not recognize Peking's claim to the island itself. There would be some confusion on this question in the near future. For the moment, however, diplomatic relations between Japan and Nationalist China would be severed. But trade would continue between them on an increasing scale through the good offices of third parties.

Some points of uncertainty need to be pondered: Had the forces of the New Imperialism anticipated the actions of Red China and Japan? If so, how far down the road had they seen? Had they become so confused or muddled they could not foresee that Japan had also prepared the way for herself to do business with an eager China, and the world, on the premise of production for the sake of production? Moreover, Japan could follow through. Her trade machinery was oiled. She had good currency and she was busily but quietly buying gold, tons of gold. And decreasing her "official" dollar holdings by rapidly spending them in America on valuable consumer goods to be used in Japan and elsewhere.

In February 1972, Nixon had termed 1971 as a "watershed year" in which United States initiatives had started a "new relationship" with the Soviet Union and had also found an "opening to China." It might be added that his initiatives had given an excuse for Japan to take its own initiatives to open roads to China as well as to the Soviet Union. Others can play the game of econopolitics, too!

The real power of the Soviet Union lies east of the Ural Mountains. It is in this area that its economic and military power are to be found. In terms of power, the Soviet Union is more Asian than European.

As for relations between the Soviet Union and Japan, they had previously signed a "declaration of peace" in 1956 but had never concluded a peace treaty formally ending the state of war that technically existed between them since World War II.

The immediate issue which prevented the signing of a formal peace treaty between them were the four islands north of Japan that were seized by Russia in World War

II. But time and delicate negotiations will solve this issue, if only to make way for larger issues. In the meantime, there is likely to be a new economic relationship of cooperation leading to large scale joint ventures in Soviet East Asia, involving oil and gas. The multinational affiliates of the corporate aristocracy will try to compete with the Japanese in these ventures with the Russians but in the end they will be frustrated and forced to withdraw.

The development of the oil reserves of the Soviet Union by Japan suggests the likelihood of a pipeline to carry oil from Siberia to the Soviet Union's Pacific Ocean coast. China will naturally watch this development with intense interest and use it as bargaining leverage against Japan.

Japan has already made her obeisances to China. And, here again, as with the Soviets, the "glue" cementing the alliance will be crude oil. The giant oil fields under the East China Sea are reserved for Japan and will be paid for in gold, services, and products.

Within this triangular affair, Japan will be very circumspect, treating both China and Russia on equal and equitable terms to avoid any misunderstandings. Diplomacy is an intangible force and good diplomacy takes time and effort. Relationships must be nursed. Communications must always remain open. Parties must meet on equal terms.

What Japan does for China she has to do for the Soviet Union. Thus, Japan must walk a tightrope, but she will be willing to take the risks for she has everything to gain and nothing to lose.

One of the risks for Japan will be that China is not likely to be easily satisfied. She will demand more trade with Japan, want more guarantees that her former northern provinces in Soviet East Asia will not be used against her by the Soviet Union. China may well use all her wiles to lure Japan away from the Soviet Union. And the latter will use all her cunning to play off America against Japan for economic bargaining purposes.

This situation could continue for a reasonable length of time, culminating in Japan's causing China and the Soviet Union to join with her in agreements opening huge economic markets stretching from East Germany to the far reaches of East Asia. These agreements would constitute in effect a military alliance between the three Asian powers. And thus would be born in this century another Axis, a Moscow-Tokyo-Peking Axis. A new gigantic Asian power bloc cemented on Moscow-Tokyo-Peking relations. Three Asian Giants!

Japan can give China and the Soviet Union the necessary tools to industrialize. China and the Soviet Union, in turn, can provide Japan with food and raw products, and an ever-increasing market.

Meanwhile, Japan can be expected to exert all efforts to get out from under the control of the Western international oil companies. Dependent on them for 99 percent of her oil, she would then increasingly have to import massive quantities of oil from the Midde East until such time as she can exploit Chinese and Russian oil reserves. And Exxon Corporation (formerly Standard Oil and owned by the Rockefeller dynasty), the world's largest international oil company, will attempt to constrain Japan from bypassing the Western oil companies. But that country will not forget its humiliation when

Nixon made his famous "U-turn" in approaching China without consulting her. Japan is a growth power, and will be the power of the twenty-first century.

The forces of the new Asian aristocracy will harass the forces of the New Imperialism. And failure of the latter to understand fully the Asian mind may well cause many errors of judgment.

The Axis will also embark on a crusade of their own, increasingly penetrating Africa and Latin America, and thereby bringing them into confrontation with the interests of the dynasty and the corporate aristocracy in Latin America.

It is in Latin America where the dynasty and the corporate aristocracy concentrated their wealth in the years prior to the crusade of the New Imperialism. And they will fight to preserve this wealth.

The top 200 U.S.-based mutinational corporations and banks which have extensive holdings in Latin America come together under the umbrella of the Rockefeller-dominated organization, the Council of the Americas.

It is in this organization that policy towards Latin America is formulated. In December 1972 after he had returned from a trip through Latin America, David Rockefeller told the Council's eighth annual meeting in New York City that "we need to know what we are before we are told what we will be allowed to become. This is certainly one of the most urgent priorities in the nation's business sector today." He was trying to deal with the criticisms which were being increasingly voiced overseas concerning his form of "economic development around the world."

4

STAGFLATION

THE waves of Campaign May had reached the shores of America. The war against the dollar in Europe was coming home to Americans in the form of high prices and social unrest.

The impact of the econostrategic and econopolitic measures of the New Imperiaism will be felt for many years in the United States. The legislative bodies of local, state, and federal government will be incapable of coping with the situation we call stagflation: the problem, previously referred to, of high inflation combined with a lack of real growth in the economy.

After two official devaluations followed by "unofficial" devaluations as a result of the floating dollar, the value of the dollar, in terms of goods and services bought, is going down and down, buying less and less.

Devaluation of the dollar is a presage of increased inflation. The burden of devaluation ultimately falls on the average working man, the pensioner, and those on fixed incomes. It erodes savings accounts, bonds, and other fixed income instruments.

It also takes more dollars for local, state, and federal programs. The dollar buys less national defense and contractors increasingly suffer cost overruns. Components for the American weapon systems manufactured abroad by the multinationals skyrocket in price. Moreover, these multinationals insist on being paid in "hard" currency, not inflated dollars.

In the longer time frame, this situation places the U.S. military establishment in an economic strait jacket. It has to return time and again to Congress for additional monies to pay domestic contractors of military hardware. The same situation prevails concerning local, state, and federal projects and participation in international financial institutions.

While a "little" inflation in the Old World era could help make the wheels of industry turn a little faster, politicians try to mislead the people by heralding the present inflation as a "new era of prosperity."

It is an Old World economic theory that inflation acts both as a subsidy to industry to generate more goods and as a protective tariff (because imported items cost more). Today, however, in the era of the multinationals, the bulk of American exports are not made entirely in America. They are made abroad and shipped to the U.S. Their cost is the same as in the Old World era: high. And because the bulk of the products consumed in America have components which come from abroad there is no incentive for American industry to generate more goods. In short, there is a lack of real growth in the American economy, and this, combined with growing inflation, tends to make business lose confidence in itself.

In this era of stagflation, the low value of the American dollar in terms of foreign exchange still further encourages the movement abroad of American industries. Which in turn means still more jobs are exported. Of course, in the early stages of stagflation, those industries in debt are able to pay off their indebtedness with cheap dollars. But, in the later stages, these same industries are apt to experience a scarcity of capital, and therefore lack the will to invest.

Stagflation distorts normal economic relationships. No true analysis can be made of the nation's standard indexes, such as the gross national product, the wholesale and retail price indexes, foreign exchange rates, stock market index, the "return" on government and other securities, or of business operations.

For accurate analysis, business would have to hire accountants who possessed the powers of a prophet and these accountants would have to be grounded in stagflation accounting. They would have to be familiar with the new tools for measuring and reducing stagflation's harmful effects. They would need to forecast the cost of raw materials, wages, capital costs, services, and they would have to be precise.

For example, how should depreciation be treated? What should be done with liquid or monetary assets, and at what cost to hold on to them? How should assets and income be treated? Understate or overstate them? What about the very important psychological barriers? Finally, should American business be required to plan from year to year instead of the usual period? And, if so, what would be the real trend in that business or industry after looking at sales, profits, dividends, and earnings per share?

With continued stagflation, financial executives, bankers, and investors have to master the techniques for analyzing the true state of company performance. They have to make accurate decisions on dividends, investments, loans, and cash management. Otherwise: stagflation for their companies, and certain destruction!

As for financial advisers, they have to be versed in stagflation analysis. Only then can they find facts which would surprise even the most sophisticated financial practitioners on the performance of apparently successful American companies.

In this age of the multinationals and giant labor unions, the economic theory of the Old World about money supply causing inflation is obsolete. What counts today is the impact—economic brinkmanship played between labor, industry, and government over the pay structure. The total demands of the labor unions during stagflation could exceed the total American economy's power to deliver. If higher wages are asked for than can be delivered, the result will be still further increases in the price levels of goods and services if the demands of the unions are to be met.

In this period of stagflation many want to know: "What can I do to protect my family financially?" Of course, if the U.S. government placed no controls or obstacles on its people, they could consider investing in multinational stocks listed in Europe which would be held for investment purposes. Perhaps at the time they are purchased in Europe, payment would have to be made in "hard" currency. If the stock were later sold, the investor would pay United States taxes on his profits in cheap dollars.

In Europe, the American investor will become acquainted with the giant multinationals listed on the various European national stock exchanges. There he will find Ford, IBM, ITT, Shell, Unilever, Sperry Rand, Chrysler, Occidental Oil, du Pont, Eastman Kodak, General Motors, and others. And increasingly the bulk of the multinationals will be buying up huge blocks of their own stocks listed on the United States stock exchanges for possible uses elsewhere during the stagflation era.

Stagflation may well destroy the effectiveness of the stock exchanges in America.

Gold would be another good investment during the era of stagflation. For over 2,500 years gold has played a monetary role and as such it has lent stability to money. The greatest advances in the economies of the world have taken place when gold itself was used as money, or when paper currency was backed or covered with gold. It should be borne in mind also that the accumulation of gold always buys the sinews of war.

However, the forces of the New Imperialism had a five-year plan to demonetize gold, to reduce it to a mere commodity. They wanted to do away with the two main functions of gold, first as the standard in terms of which par values of currencies were expressed and, secondly, as a major reserve unit. They have succeeded for the time being in abolishing both functions. And in so doing they have brought about stagflation.

For those who would speculate in gold stocks, the following new rules should be noted during the era of stagflation and the paper dollar: If there were a free gold market in a world system of monetized gold (gold backing for currency), then any attempt to reduce the price of free gold by its sale would succeed. On the other hand, if there were a free gold market in a world system of demonetized gold or what would amount to a world system of demonetized gold (e.g., when America "induced" Europe not to exchange dollars for gold after the estabishment of a two-tier gold standard in the 1967/1968 period), then any attempt to reduce the price of free gold by its sale would fail. Its price would rise.

Further, if Europe were on a monetized gold standard and America was not, then Europeans would have no need to hold gold stocks. Americans would—if their government afforded them the right to hold it by law. Rest assured, however, that in such an event, the bulk of America's official gold stock would go into the coffers of the combined forces of the New Imperialism. They have worked and planned many years for this! The people would only have "crumbs"—the old U.S. or new gold coins from Europe in "unlimited" supply.

The forces of the New Imperialism will hold their gold during the entire era of stagflation and then resell it to the United States government at a tremendous windfall profit when America is forced back on a monetized gold system. They will have by that time forced the price of gold up to six or seven times its official price set in 1934! This is a part of their second five-year plan.

If the world monetary system should return to gold as a cover for their currencies, then monetary gold could be allowed to reflect the reality of the times so far as the price level of goods and services are concerned. If allowed to play its proper role it would return stability to the international monetary system.

Increasingly the price of gold would reflect the reality of the times. However, not six or seven times the 1934 price! That would be unrealistic, and would contribute further to stagflation. If the price of gold were raised to equate the *real* advance in the price of other commodities since 1934, that should suffice to stop stagflation and take the Western world well into the twenty-first century. The free gold market would then be closed because in time the official and private market price of gold would be narrowed or even eliminated.

True, any price increase of gold would tend to stimulate expectations of further changes. However, once clear, concerted actions were taken against further increases in the official price of gold, any such expectations would be totally eliminated.

The revaluation of gold and linking it once again to currency would not, alone, be sufficient to create a new and improved international monetary system. The system, at the minimum, would have to be tied to a firm, fixed price of gold, and as the diversity of economic development evolved, partial agreements could be entered into to take care of any new developments. At the maximum, then, it would be flexible.

During the period of stagflation in America, the executive machinery of the federal government will be busy trying to ward off attacks on the multinationals of the corporate aristocracy.

The multinational corporations came to the attention of the American public in 1972 as a result of the infamous

ITT-Chile affair. ITT had tried to interfere in a political decision in Chile by using its client followers in the executive branch of the American government.

It had not lived up to its own words which appeared in its 1971 annual report: "A corporation exists by public acceptance." Or this from its full-page advertisement which was printed in red, white, and blue in the official program for the thirty-sixth quadrennial national nominating convention of the Democratic Party July 10–13, 1972, at Miami Beach, Florida: " 'The time at which I stand before you is full of interest. The eyes of all nations are fixed on our Republic. . . . Great is the stake placed in our hands; great is the responsibility which must rest upon the people of the United States. Let us realize the importance of the attitude in which we stand before the world.'—Andrew Jackson." Hardly any statement could have been more spectacularly calculated to mislead.

The situation would best be described in the words of an editorial which appeared in one of the leading newspapers in America: "Here is exactly the kind of brazen behavior on the international scene that has given a bad name to giant American business firms. . . . No Marxist critics, whether at home, Chile or elsewhere, could inflict half as much damage on the standing of American international corporations or half as much discredit on the free enterprise system as had ITT's own behavior. . . . Thus if ITT has furnished ample material for a book on how a giant corporation should not behave in the last half of the twentieth century, the Administration has supplied the stuff for a chapter on the pitfalls of a close relationship between such a firm and the Government."

ITT is a good example of a multinational corporation. It is a part of the corporate aristocracy. In Europe alone its total amount of business for 1971 amounted to some $2.5 billion! And its officials in New York City would always consider Europe as "a choice target for further acquisitions."

Had a multinational corporation gone too far in attempting to shuttle $1 million to a foreign country via the executive machinery of the American government in an obvious attempt to thwart a political decision taken by the citizens of a foreign country? If a member of the corporate aristocracy had tried in this instance, and was caught, how many other attempts have succeeded? Inevitably, Europe would be asking these questions.

President Salvador Allende Gossens said the CIA had worked with ITT to try to block his election in 1970. Chile would not pay "even half a cent to this multinational company which was on the verge of plunging Chile into civil war," he declared. He also accused "imperialist" corporations of fomenting wars, worldwide inflation, and of dominating the economies of underdeveloped countries. He mentioned the Anaconda Company and the Kennecott Copper Corporation, whose multimillion-dollar assets in Chile have been nationalized. Dr. Allende said Chile's dispute was not with "the people or the workers of the U.S.," but with the U.S. government and international corporations. "Here in Chile, we do not use the term 'Yankee go home,' " he said. "We say, 'Imperialists go home.' "

The United States Congress was replete with committees investigating the effects of multinationals like

ITT on the economic and foreign relations of the United States. To defend the multinationals, the corporate aristocracy caused Peter M. Flanigan, executive director of the Council on International Economic Policy and an assistant to President Nixon to appear before Congressional committees. In his testimony defending the conduct of the multinational corporations, he said they had not "exported jobs" and had been a "major help" to the nation's balance of payments! Quoting verbatim: *"In general, it is difficult to find much evidence* that the multinational corporations, *as a group,* have damaged the United States economy or its workers." (Emphasis added.)

This statement is a classic example of the use of "weasel words" meant to be intentionally ambiguous. It should read: "There is specific evidence to prove that the United States economy and its workers have been damaged." As for stagflation, Mr. Flanigan had specific evidence that the major multinationals had done great harm to the economy and its workers. But such evidence was never presented.

Mr. Flanigan, widely regarded as a string-puller for blue chip businesses with problems, and known around the White House as "Rockefeller's and Dillon's Man," testified further that "no Administration position has been reached" on possible changes in the taxation of corporate income earned abroad. He indicated a reluctance to accept any major changes that would place U.S.-based multinationals at a "disadvantage" with their foreign-owned competitors, such as requiring them to pay taxes on foreign earnings when earned rather than, as now, when remitted to the United States.

How the payment of United States taxes would be a "disadvantage" to U.S.-based corporations was never explained. Mr. Flanigan knew that the bulk of more than $80 billion in excess liquidity was owned by the multinational affiliates abroad. He knew these same multinationals had earned over $10 billion in 1972 from their European operations alone and their estimated earnings there in 1973 would be well in excess of $15 billion.

But the U.S.-based multinational corporations do not want to pay taxes on the earnings of their foreign affiliates. Any attempt by legislation to make them do so would be met with the line that such legislation would be "completely out of context with the time and age we live in. *The kind of world most of us want to live in, where the chances of another world war are minimized, is an integrated world.*" (Emphasis added.)

These are the recent (1973) words of Constant van Vlierden, a native of The Netherlands, and executive vice-president, International, of Bank of America, San Francisco. It must be noted that Prince Bernhard of The Netherlands *and his associates* hold the same "integrated world" philosophy.

Thus, in a one world or integrated world, U.S.-based multinational corporations would not pay U.S. taxes on the earnings of their foreign affiliates! And, as one U.S. congressman from Georgia said, if "we hit the multinationals too hard, they'll simply shed their U.S. citizenship and get foreign charters."

91

An American citizen working abroad must pay United States taxes whether his income is remitted to the United States or not. Why not apply the same principle to U.S.-based corporations doing business abroad through their foreign affiliates? They should not be expected to reap the benefits and not take the detriments. If these multi-nationals were taxed on their income earned abroad the tax load on the average working man and woman in America would be substantially reduced and there would be no such thing as a balance of payments deficit for the United States! As it is, the American taxpayer is subsidizing these corporations in exporting jobs! These corporations are therefore themselves on a form of welfare.

In 1973, David Rockefeller had these words to say: "Corporations must develop more effective tools for measuring the social, as well as economic costs and benefits of their actions. . . . Businessmen must take the initiative to spell out more clearly and positively the longer-range economic and technical implications of current proposals for social problem-solving. . . . We must press forward on the national level to create broader and more viable long-range goals, to assess what business can and cannot do to meet these goals, and to set more comprehensive strategies to combine the strengths of public and private resources."

David Rockefeller's words bespeak lofty ideals. It is difficult to understand, therefore, why he and his corporate aristocracy client followers do not put them into practice. Are they meant merely to delude? Nowhere in Mr. Rockefeller's writings can we find that he supported gold as backing for the dollar. As a Harvard economics professor and a Nobel Prize winner said: "It would not conform to *our* idea of a flexible and evolving form of capitalism." (Emphasis added.)

Meanwhile, the United States, under prodding from American labor, would increasingly be turning inward, isolationist, and protectionist.

Most of the families of the corporate aristocracy would move to Europe where new resources would be available to them.

What would be left for the American people during the stagflation era in a service-oriented economy? High taxes, unemployment, crime and addiction, decaying cities, a collapsing educational system, a break-up of family life, experiments with avant-garde religions, and so forth.

And what of Europe? Ambassador Watson (IBM corporate aristocracy) would say: "Europe is flourishing, it is beautiful."

During this period of stagflation America would also be engaged in East-West trade. Credit facilities would be stretched to the breaking point. All the client followers of the corporate aristocracy including the dynasty itself would exhort the Export-Import Bank of the United States to extend credit to its foreign buyers.

The Export-Import Bank of the United States (Eximbank) was first established by executive order of President Roosevelt in 1934 to help develop trade between the United States and the Soviet Union. At that time, the United States had only recently extended diplomatic recognition to the Soviet Union. However, no trade on credit took place then between the parties; this would happen forty years later under a Republican administration.

Eximbank went on to do a good job in helping United States exporters to sell their products abroad by extending credit to foreign buyers. It had a good record in its banking operations. Although an independent agency of the United States government, it was made to finance the sale of military equipment during the Kennedy and Johnson administrations. During this time Eximbank also caused participation certificates to be issued to favored institutional investors in the United States and abroad to raise funds. Congress did not fund the bank although it was bound by government budget limitations.

Eximbank is a very important tool for the forces of the New Imperialism. They can force it to borrow huge dollar amounts from the U.S. Treasury in order to finance East-West trade. This means borrowing the money of the American taxpayers from the United States Treasury at a rate of interest more than it would lend to the countries involved in East-West trade.

Eximbank may have outstanding at any one time, loans, guarantees, and insurance on loans aggregating $27.5 billion! If this figure could be translated into "assets," the bank would come in third of the top twenty banks in the world with Bank of America first, First National City Corporation of New York second, and Chase Manhattan Corporation fourth. The Barclays Bank Group would be fifth.

The bulk of the programs administered by Eximbank assists the corporate aristocracy in its export sales on a credit basis. While these export sales do sustain employ-

ment in certain specialized areas, there is no actual benefit to employment at large. The bulk of these programs
benefit multinational banks and harm the Old World
theory of balance of payments. If and when foreign
buyers repay loans in a stagflation era, they will be
repaying in "soft" dollars.

Here is another instance where the corporate aristocracy
is being subsidized to export jobs. Although the products
exported must be manufactured in the United States, it
would increasingly be found that the bulk of the exports
would have been manufactured in Europe or Japan, or
the bulk of components would be manufactured abroad,
exported to America for assembly, and then reshipped
abroad to the foreign buyers. This would be completely
contrary to the sole purpose of the Eximbank: to finance
the export of U.S.-made products.

A flagrant example of stretching the usual banking
terms of Eximbank is the financing of a plant to produce
trucks and engines on the Kama River in the town of
Naberejnaya Chelny, 550 miles east of Moscow. This
financing was approved March 21, 1973.

Eximbank's usual length of term for loans range from
three to five, or seven years for a limited class of products.
However, the repayment period for this loan is 12 years
with a grace period of 4½ years; in effect, a total of 16½
years before the first repayment is made!

The government of the Soviet Union guarantees to
Eximbank its credits extended or guaranteed by Eximbank to the Bank for Foreign Trade of the U.S.S.R.
(Vneshtorgbank). Normally, credits extended by Eximbank are deposited in United States banks where the

foreign importer draws on the credit to pay the American exporter. Not in this case, however. Eximbank's portion of the money will be deposited directly into the coffers of the Vneshtorgbank in Moscow.

Participating, too, in the overall loan of $192.1 million is Chase Manhattan Bank. Chase provided $86.4 million guaranteed by the Ministry of Foreign Trade of the U.S.S.R. Eximbank charged 6 percent interest but Chase will not make public its terms for its part of the overall loan. Some American bankers suspect that Chase's interest rate is somewhat lower than Eximbank's 6 percent rate. If true, this would beat Chase's competitors for this type of banking business.

Eximbank credit facilities will be used for many such projects in the East-West trade shuttle during the stagflation era. To accomplish this it will have to dip into its reserves! In addition, billions of taxpayer dollars will be used for such East-West trade. Thus Americans have been put into the same shoes as those in the developing Third World nations which had voted for the admission of China into the United Nations only to find that they had cut themselves off from the benefits of the specialized agencies of the United Nations. As a result of these so-called loans by the executive machinery of the American government, the social programs in America to help the American people will be curtailed drastically for the benefit of the Soviet Union, China, and East European trade. Huge exports of wheat and other agricultural commodities to these countries will cause some food shortages, transport dislocations, and greatly increased costs in business activity. However, the cost of oil products will soar because their prices are arbitrarily established by the dynasty and the corporate aristocracy. A gallon of gasoline, for example, will cost at least three or four times its 1972 price in the second five-year plan period. The stagflation period.

To assist in this travesty, an office in the United States Commerce Department will be invented to "stimulate" East-West trade, using Eximbank as an abyss for dollars.

Stagflation and East-West trade could eventually cause Eximbank to close its doors. And with it would go the foreign trade programs administered by the Domestic International Sales Corporation, Overseas Private Investment Corporation, Private Export Funding Corporation, Foreign Credit Insurance Association, Commodity Credit Corporation Credit Sales Program, Private Investment Center of the Agency for International Development, and other incentive programs supported directly or indirectly by the American taxpayer.

EPILOGUE

———

WHAT has been observed in the preceding chapters has been the power of the combined forces of the dynasty and its client followers to bend America to the purpose of establishing an empire abroad.

It is questionable, however, if such power will suffice to overcome the countermeasures of the young industrialists of Europe. The multinational affiliates of the American corporate aristocracy will offer resistance, but ultimately will have to be content to be "good citizens" of Europe, severing all ties with the forces of the New Imperialism.

The assets in the name of the multinational affiliates will remain in Europe, and their accumulated profits will never be taxed by the United States government.

Cooperation with the forces of the New Imperialism had come to mean domination by these forces. Said U.S. Ambassador Arthur K. Watson (IBM corporate aristocracy), bidding farewell to the American community in Paris in 1972: "I believe the will on both sides [Europe and America] is for cooperation, not confrontation. Certainly this is in the best interests of both Europe and America. While it has been said time and again for almost thirty years, it is worth saying again that my nation's foreign policy favors an economically strong and politically and militarily cohesive Europe." The words were pleasant enough, yet the actions of the dynasty and all of its client followers belied them. Their actions did not, in the words of President Pompidou of France, lead to a "factor of balance."

The actions of the New Imperialism—the external threat to Europe—will eventually cause Europe to unite much quicker than it had planned.

As steps toward this unity Europe will adopt the following interim measures:

—The central banks will cease to operate in the Eurodollar market.

—The billions of dollars in Europe will be mopped up by giving Eurobonds with a reasonably fixed rate of interest to the multinational affiliates.

—The imposition of a two-tier (two-market) system— one rate of exchange reasonably fixed for commercial transactions, another system subject to the free market forces of supply and demand for capital transactions. This would help preserve the commercial rates from being swamped by any so-called speculative movements of capital.

These measures will give Europe a breather before the next crisis—a world monetary crisis of such proportions that will cause Europe to establish her own common currency backed by gold—a monetized gold system.

As for America, she will go her own way pushed by the momentum of the New Imperialism. She will enter the tunnel of the Big Trade War with all of its self-protective devices. The free trade idea will have gasped its last breath. Then the three large trading blocs, America, Europe, and the New Axis, will turn their politicians, bureaucrats, and diplomats into traveling salesmen busy taking orders from the leaders of the Third World and each other.

Credit facilities for America during this period of stagflation will be stretched to the breaking point but in the end Japan will be the victor because she has exercised and conditioned herself to win any trade war on the premise of production for the sake of production.

The United States presence in the Panama Canal Zone area is a geostrategic necessity to insure shipping through the canal. It will also become a geostrategic necessity for the new Asian aristocracy, just as Europe became for the New Imperialism.

If the new Asian forces are not understood, but are met with ignorance and arrogance, then the world will indeed be headed not for a "generation of peace" of which President Nixon has so proudly boasted, but for World War III.

INDEX

Africa, 77
Allende Gossens, Salvador, 89
Allied Chemical Corporation, 54
American Gold Association, 29
American Machine and Foundry
    Company, 17
Anaconda Company, 89
Atlantic Richfield Company, 51

Bank for Foreign Trade of the
    U.S.S.R. (Vneshtorgbank),
    95–96
Bank of America, 91, 94
Barclays Bank Group, 94
Bass, Perry, 54
Bernhard, Prince of the Nether-
    lands, 34, 91
Bretton Woods Agreement
    (1944), 26, 41, 55, 60–61
Brookings Institution, 17
Brown & Root, Inc., 54
Brown, George, 54
Butcher, Willard C., 17

Campaign May, 32–35, 42, 81
Caterpillar Tractor Company, 51
Central Intelligence Agency, 89
Chase Manhattan Bank, 15–19,
    42, 52–54, 62, 96
Chase Manhattan Corporation,
    17, 34, 94
    International Advisory Commit-
    tee, 34, 43

Chase Manhattan Overseas Bank-
    ing Corporation, 17
Chile, 88–89
China-America Tade Council, 70–
    71
China, Peoples Republic of, 37,
    96
    Chase Manhattan Bank, 52
    diplomatic relations with Japan,
    71–76
    Moscow-Tokyo-Peking Axis, 75–
    77, 103
    Nixon visit, 68–70, 72, 74, 76–
    77
    U.N. admission, 69
Chou En-lai, 73
Chrysler Corporation, 18, 31, 85
Columbia Broadcasting System,
    Inc., 19
Committee for Economic Devel-
    opment, 18
Commodity Credit Corporation
    Credit Sales Program, 97
Connally, John B., Jr., 13, 42–
    50, 53–54, 58
Connor, John T., 54
Corporate aristocracy
    client-followers of, 12–14, 24,
    57, 59
    econostrategy, 42–48
    European investment, 25–26,
    35, 37–38
    European opposition, 63
    go-betweens, 16–18

Index

Corporate aristocracy (*Cont.*)
  Latin American investment, 77
  oil, 54, 96–97
  productive capacity, 68
  Texas, 53–54
  Versailles conference, 51
  See also Multinational corporations
Council of the Americas, 77
Council on International Economic Policy, 90
Council on Foreign Relations, 16, 18, 54, 68, 72
Credito Italiano, 52

Deutsche mark, 59
Dillon, C. Douglas, 13, 18, 28, 43, 90
Dillon, Read & Company, 18
Dollar (U.S.)
  convertibility, 30
  devaluation, 36–37, 45, 47–50, 57–59, 81–82
  "dollar crisis," 23, 47, 59, 61
  fixed exchange rates, 45, 60
  float, 33, 44–46, 57, 61, 81
  inflow into Europe, 26, 32, 42, 44–45, 56–57, 102
  "paper" currency, 67–68
  reserve currency, 50, 68
  severance from gold, 26–29, 36–37, 41, 44–47, 58–59, 61, 67, 85–86
  "soft" dollars, 26, 33, 35, 37
  speculation, 36, 59, 84
  supports, 23, 27–28, 33, 45–46
Domestic International Sales Corporation, 97
DuPont de Nemours & Company, 51, 85

Eastman Kodak Company, 51, 85
Econopolitics, 67–77
Econostrategy, 41–63, 67
England, 34
Eurobonds, 102
Eurodollars, 102

Export-Import Bank of the U.S. (Eximbank), 52, 93–97
Exxon Corporation, 51, 76

Federated Department Stores, 18
First National City Bank Corporation of N.Y., 94
Flanigan, Peter M., 18, 90–91
FMC Corporation, 18
Ford Foundation, 12
Ford Motor Company, 12, 24, 31, 34, 56, 85
Foreign Credit Insurance Association, 97
Franks, Oliver, 28

General Electric Company, 18, 51
General Motors Corporation, 12, 24, 34, 51, 56, 85
Geostrategy, 23–38, 103
Gold
  demonetized, 26–29, 36–37, 41, 44–47, 58–59, 61, 67, 85–86
  "free" market price, 26–27, 85–87
  monetized, 86, 102
  official price, 26–28, 47, 49–50, 58, 85
  "paper gold", 59
  revaluation, 86–87
  reserves, 27–28, 50, 85
  speculation, 32, 58–59, 85–86
  two-tier market system, 27, 86, 102
Goodyear Tire & Rubber Company, 51
Grey-Poup-on-Maille, 34
Guinard, 34

Haldeman, H.R., 13
Heinz, H.J., 34, 51
Hewlett-Packard Company, 17–18
Hewlett, William R., 17–18
Hogg, Ima, 54
Holland, 34
Hunt, N. Bunker, 54
Hunt Oil Company, 54

108

Industrial Development Organization, 69
Industrial Revolution, 15
Inflation theory, 82, 84
"Integrated world" philosophy, 91
International Business Machines Corporation, 12, 24, 34, 37, 46, 51, 54, 56, 85, 101
International Telephone and Telegraph Corporation, 12, 24, 34, 51, 85, 89–90
Chile affair, 87–89

Japan, 23–24, 45–46, 48, 57, 103
crude oil, 75–76
diplomatic relations with China, 71–76
diplomatic relations with Soviet Union, 73–76
Moscow-Tokyo-Peking Axis, 75–77, 103
Nixon visit to China, 72, 76–77
Jeumont-Schneider, 34
Johnson, Lyndon B., 44, 54, 94

Kennecott Copper Corporation, 89
Kennedy, John F., 27–28, 94
Kern County Land Company, 18
Kissinger, Henry, 14, 19, 34, 62, 72

Labor unions, 25, 44, 84
Latin America, 58–59, 77. See *also* Chile
Lazarus, Ralph, 18
Lazarus, Steven, 18
Lenin, V.I., 14
Lloyds Bank Ltd., 28
Lodge, Henry Cabot, 69
London School of Economics, 15
Loudon, John Hugo J., 17

Marshall Plan, 24
Meany, George, 19
Merck & Company, 51
Mitsubishi Bank, 52

Moncrief, W.A., 54
Multinational corporations
affiliates, 24–25, 30–36, 50–51, 56–57, 91, 101–102
Campaign May, 32–35
commodity market, 58–59
currency speculation, 35–37
definition of, 24–25
exports, 82
ITT-Chile affair, 87–89
Latin America, 58–59, 77
shuttle operations, 30–32
stagflation, 82–85, 87, 90
U.S. taxes, 32, 84, 90–92, 101
Murchison, John, 54
Museum of Modern Art of New York, 17

National Committee on U.S.-China Relations, Inc., 18
National Westminster Bank, 52–53
Nederlandsche Crediet Bank, N.V., 17
New Imperialism, 15, 38, 51–52, 57, 77, 101–103
Campaign May, 32–35, 42, 81
Eximbank, 94
five-year plan to demonetize gold, 26–28, 37, 42, 61–62, 85
Nixon, Richard, 45, 54–60, 62–63
stagflation, 85–86
twin objectives, 67
Nixon, Richard M., 14, 19, 38, 49–50, 59–63, 103
Democrats for Nixon, 54
New Economic Program, 41–46
relationship with John Connally, 48, 53–56
visit to China, 68–70, 72, 77
visit to Soviet Union, 71–72

Occidental Oil, 85
Oil, cost of, 96–97
Orion Bank, Ltd., 52–53

Index

Overseas Private Investment Corporation, 97

Panama Canal Zone, 103
Paris Agreement (1973), 61
Patterson, Herbert P., 17
Perot, H. Ross, 54
Pfizer, Inc., 51
Pompidou, George, 102
Private Export Funding Corporation, 97
Private Investment Center of the Agency for International Development, 97

Rand Corporation, 18
Rockefeller, David, 14–17, 19, 34, 55–56, 90, 92
    on capitalism, 14–15
    Council of the Americas, 77
    Smithsonian Agreement, 49
    Versailles Conference, 51
Rockefeller dynasty, 11–16, 19, 49, 70, 76, 97, 101
Rockefeller Foundation, 18–19, 28, 43, 54, 68, 72
Rockefeller, John D., 11, 12, 15
Rockefeller, John D., Jr., 16
Rockefeller, Nelson, 19, 72
Roosa, Robert V., 67–68
Roosevelt, Franklin D., 93
Royal Bank of Canada, 52
Royal Dutch Petroleum Company, 12, 17, 34, 51, 54, 85
Russia. See Soviet Union

Sato, Eisaku, 72–73
Schiller, Karl, 34, 48
Scott Paper Company, 18
Shell Petroleum Company, Ltd. See Royal Dutch Petroleum Company
Shultz, George P., 13, 55–56, 58, 62
Sid Richardson Estate, 54
Smithsonian Agreement (1971), 49, 55–57
Société Génerale de Belgique, 34

Soviet Union, 36–37, 63
    Chase Manhattan Bank, 52, 96
    diplomatic relations with Japan, 73–76
    Eximbank loans, 93–96
    Moscow-Tokyo-Peking Axis, 75–77, 103
    Vneshtorgbank, 95–96
    wheat sale by U.S., 71–72, 96
Sperry Rand Corporation, 85
"Spirit of the New Imperialism." See New Imperialism
Stagflation, 43, 81–97, 103
Standard Oil Company, Indiana, 51
Stanton, Frank, 19

Taiwan, 69, 73
Tanaka, Kakuei, 72–73

Unilever, 12, 34, 56, 85
United Nations, 69, 96
University of Chicago, 15, 18–19
U.S. and Foreign Securities Corporation, 18

Van Vlierden, Constant, 91
Versailles Conference (1972), 51, 53
Vneshtorgbank (U.S.S.R.), 95–96
Volcker, Paul A., 13, 19, 42, 47–49, 57

Watson, Arthur K., 37, 46, 93, 101–102
Watson, Thomas J., Jr., 54
Westdeutsche Landesbank Girozentrale, 52–53
Westinghouse Electric Corporation, 34, 51
World Bank, 69
World Health Organization, 69

Xerox Corporation, 51

Ziegler, Ronald, 13